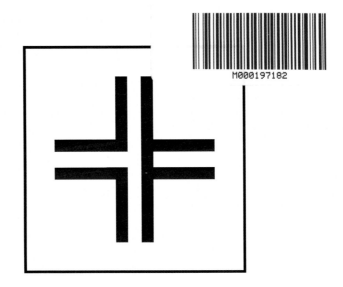

PARENT/CHILD
DEDICATION SERVICE
SUNDAY | OCTOBER 4, 2015

"Train up a child in the way he should go;
even when he is old he will not depart
from it."

Proverbs 22:6

CHURCH at THE CROSS
GRAPEVINE, TX

LUCY MICHELE BENDER

Lucy - Light
Michele - Gift from God

"For this reason I bow my knees before the Father, from whom every family in heaven and on earth is named, that according to the riches of his glory he may grant you to be strengthened with power through his Spirit in your inner being, so that Christ may dwell in your hearts through faith—that you, being rooted and grounded in love... Eph.3:14-19

AUGUST 13, 2015
TO DAVID & MEAGAN

EMMA GRACE HIMES

Grace - God's unmerited favor

His eye is on the sparrow; and I know He watches over me. Matt. 10:29-31

AUGUST 14, 2015
TO STEPHEN & MELODY

ELLIOT JAMES McEWIN

Elliot - Jehovah is God

I have no greater joy than to hear that my children are walking in the truth. 3 John 1:4

NOVEMBER 21, 2015
TO AARON & VALERIE

CHURCH at THE CROSS

We are glad you've joined us today, and we hope you feel loved and encouraged while you're here. We strive to be a hospitable people who show the same gracious welcome to others that Jesus has shown to us.

CONNECT

To learn more about CATC, stop by our Connection Center in the Atrium. We have information on what it means to be a Christ-follower or about baptism. You can learn about membership or how to become a part of a Life Group. We can connect you with service opportunities or have someone pray with you. We're here to help.

LIFE GROUPS

At CATC, we aspire to be a family of gospel communities ordering our everyday lives together around Jesus and his mission. We see Life Groups as one of the primary avenues for this to happen. Life Groups are available on and off campus on Sundays and weeknights. Visit the Connection Center to learn more.

CHILDREN & STUDENTS

Kids at the Cross meets in our KidsTown facility and is for birth–6th grade. Birth–4th grade meet during both services on Sunday mornings. Life Groups for 5th–6th grades meet in the Loft at 9am and are encouraged to attend the 10:30am gathering with their family. Visit the Red Desk on the second floor of KidsTown for more info.

Students at the Cross seeks to provide gospel community where all 7th-12th graders can be discipled and experience renewal in Jesus. Sundays at 9am in the Hangar, students can be a part of a Student Life Group. Discipleship Groups meet weekly off campus at various times. Our Arise worship gathering is on the first Wednesday of the month at 7pm in the Hangar. Visit the Hangar to learn more about how to get your student involved.

#CALLTORENEWAL

3000 WLM D. TATE | GRAPEVINE, TX | 817.488.8533 | CHURCHATTHECROSS.COM

A WORD OF AFFIRMATION

I have told you these things, so that in me you may have peace. In this world you will have trouble. But take heart! I have overcome the world.

– John 16:33

DAILY BIBLE READING

Sunday, October 4
Ps 118, 145 | 2 Kng 20:1-21 | Acts 12:1-17 | Luke 7:11-17

Monday, October 5
Ps 121-126 | 2 Kng 22:1-13 | 1 Cor 11:2, 17-22 | Matt 9:1-8

Tuesday, October 6
Ps 97, 99, 100, 94, 95 | 2 Ch 29:1-3, 30:1-27 | 1 Cor 7:32-40 | Matt 7:1-12

Wednesday, October 7
Ps 119:145-176, 128-130 | 2 Kng 22:14-23:3 | 1 Cor 11:23-34 | Matt 9:9-17

Thursday, October 8
Ps 131-135 | 2 Kng 23:4-25 | 1 Cor 12:1-11 | Matt 9:18-26

Friday, October 9
Ps 140-143 | 2 Kng 23:36-24:17 | 1 Cor 12:12-26 | Matt 9:27-34

Saturday, October 10
Ps 137, 144, 104 | Jer 35:1-19 | 1 Cor 12:27-13:3 | Matt 9:35-10:4

Sunday, October 11
Ps 146, 147, 111, 112, 113 | Jer 36:1-10 | Acts 14:8-18 | Luke 7:36-50

ANNOUNCEMENTS

Grow: Basics of Christian Living *Oct. 4–Nov. 8 | 10:30am | Port. Rm. 1*
Grow is a six-week class focused on learning the basics of Christian living. It is designed for new Christians or those who simply need a refresher course on spiritual growth. Join us in learning to experience growth in the new life we have in Jesus. You can register online at *churchatthecross.com/calendar.*

Equipping at the Cross *Monday | Oct. 5 | 6pm | Worship Center*
Pastor JR Vassar will lead a men's forum and author and speaker Jen Wilkin will lead a women's forum on the destructive nature of pornography and the Church's responsibility to those who suffer with it. This fall, we also offer a curriculum for birth–6th grade on developing a deeper prayer life based on the Lord's prayer. Please register your children online at *churchatthecross.com/calendar.*

Gospel & Baptism Class for Kids *Sunday | Oct. 11 | 10:30am | the Loft*
This class is for children and their parents who have questions pertaining to what we believe about baptism here at Church at the Cross and what next steps they need to follow. For more information, email lori@churchatthecross.com.

Hall's Pumpkin Farm *Tuesday | Oct. 13 | 6-8pm*
Grab your Life Group, friends, and family and join us for our annual night at Hall's Pumpkin Farm located at 3420 Hall Johnson Rd on Tuesday, October 13 from 6-8pm. Enjoy the corn maze, hayride, food, and pumpkins! The maze is $5, hayride $3, or both for $6. The farm has barbecue for sale. The church will provide cookies.

Night of Prayer *Sunday | October 18 | 5pm | Worship Center*
Join us for a night dedicated to worship and prayer. This is a time to practice our collective calling to intercede on behalf of our local church, our community and the world, crying out to God for people and places to experience renewal in Jesus. Childcare is provided for birth–4th grade, please register online for childcare at *churchatthecross.com/calendar.*

NATHAN KYLE McEWIN

Nathan - Gift from God

For this child I prayed, and the Lord has granted me my petition that I made to him. Therefore I have lent him to the Lord. As long as he lives, he is lent to the Lord." And he worshiped the Lord there. 1 Sam. 1:27-28

NOVEMBER 21, 2015
TO AARON & VALERIE

IRIS HOSANNA SAUNDERS

Iris - Kristen's grandmother
Hosanna - Joyful noice of praise

For this reason, since the day we heard about you, we have not stopped praying for you. We continually ask God to fill you with the knowledge of his will through all the wisdom and understanding that the Spirit gives, so that you may live a life worthy of the Lord and please him in every way: bearing fruit in every good work, growing in the knowledge of God. Col. 1:9-10

MARCH 25, 2014
TO SCOTT & KRISTEN

SAVANNAH GRACE STRAWN

Grace - God's unmerited favor

For this child I prayed, and the Lord has granted me my petition that I made to him. So now I give him to the Lord. For his whole life l be given over to the lord. 1 Sam. 1:27-28

SEPTEMBER 25, 2007
TO CURTIS & JANE

DEDICATION COMMITMENTS

TO THE PARENTS:

Do you promise to love the Lord your God with all your heart, mind, soul, and strength and demonstrate to your children with your life that Jesus is the object of your greatest trust and your greatest treasure?

Do you promise to treasure one another in covenant love and loyalty, seeking to grow in your marriage so as to provide a secure and loving home for your children?

Do you promise to pray for and over your children and to teach them the Word of God so that they grow up with a rich knowledge of the gospel?

Do you promise to seek God's wisdom in the training and discipline of your children and to repent toward them when your discipline lacks love, self-control, and gospel hope?

Do you promise to seek to instill in your children a proper love for and enjoyment of this world and to model for your children what it means to live on mission with God in it?

TO THE CHURCH:

Will you, the church, promise to join them in the promises with your prayers, encouragement, and accountability?

THANK YOU FOR PARTICIPATING IN THIS SPECIAL SERVICE

Rebecca Manley Pippert

grow

Your life with Christ

LIVE | **GROW** | KNOW

Grow

© Rebecca Manley Pippert, 2015

Published by
The Good Book Company
Tel (UK): 0333 123 0880
International: +44 (0) 208 942 0880
Email: info@thegoodbook.co.uk

Websites:
North America: www.thegoodbook.com
UK: www.thegoodbook.co.uk
Australia: www.thegoodbook.com.au
New Zealand: www.thegoodbook.co.nz

ISBN: 9781910307403

Published in association with the literary agency of Wolgemuth and Associates, Inc.

Printed in the Czech Republic
Design by André Parker

Contents

Introduction 5

How To Use This Booklet 7

1. What Is God's Plan For My life? 9

2. Growing Together In Christ 19

3. Why Pray When We Can Worry Instead? 29

4. Walking In Obedience 41

5. Talking About God Without Sounding Religious 51

Useful Resources 61

Introduction

God does not want us just to keep going as Christians. He wants us to enjoy *growing* as Christians.

But what does growing as a Christian actually mean? Is it just about improving ourselves through our own efforts, or is it more exciting than that? What are we growing into? And how does it all happen?

New believers often find getting to grips with the Christian life quite daunting. And many of us who have been Christians a while longer feel we're stuck in a rut, or that our faith has become a routine. Going to church, reading the Bible, praying to God and living Christ's way can so easily become things we do dutifully... or don't do at all.

This is why I have written GROW—and why I'm so thrilled that you're reading this! Christian growth is more wonderful and life-changing than we often really grasp. God has given us ways in which to change and be changed. We just need to understand, appreciate and enjoy them. And that's what this five-week course is designed to enable you to do, individually and as a group.

All children grow. And since all Christians are children of our heavenly Father, we must grow too. So whoever you are, and whatever stage of your journey you're at, GROW is for you. As I've written it, I've been so excited to see what it is that God wants for us and what he does for us. I'm praying that session by session, you'll find yourself filled with that same excitement.

I hope that together we'll not only be encouraged to keep going, but to keep growing.

Becky

How To Use This Handbook

Everything you'll need (apart from a Bible and a pen) is in this booklet. Each session has several different elements:

 Introduction. Helps you begin to think about the main theme of the session. You can read in the booklet, or watch Becky on the DVD or download.

 Historical Context. Explains what is going on in the part of the Bible you're about to look at.

 Bible Study. This will take most of your time, as you look at the Bible together and share what you discover as you answer the questions in this booklet. A good Bible translation to use is the "NIV2011." There is space in the booklet to make notes, but it's not compulsory!

 Live What You Learn. The Bible changes us in how we think and act. This section encourages you to think about what difference the section of the Bible you've been reading might make to you.

 Life Stories. Listen to people sharing some of their story about how and why they became a Christian, or what life as a Christian has been like for them.

 Following Jesus. Listen to Becky talk about the main themes of the session. There is a summary of what she says in your booklet.

 Praying Together. A time to speak to God. Prayers don't have to be long or use complicated words; and feel free to pray silently in your head if you don't feel comfortable praying out loud.

 Going Deeper. Something for you to take home to read and think about between sessions. This is entirely optional. If you have any questions, do ask them at the start of the next session.

Note For Leaders: You'll find a concise Leader's Guide for the course, as well as the downloadable videos, at www.thegoodbook.com/grow. You'll need the access code in your DVD case to be able to get onto the page.

I. What Is God's Plan For My Life?

Romans 8 v 14-17 and v 28-29

There are two things that are important to understand once we become Christians. First: *Who am I now that I belong to Christ? How does God see me?* And second: *What does God plan to do in my life?*

Romans chapter 8, which is widely regarded as one of the greatest chapters in all of Scripture, addresses those very questions. *How does God see me?* "There is now no condemnation for those who are in Christ Jesus" (Romans 8 v 1); the chapter ends with the assurance that nothing can separate us from the love of God in Christ.

Why can we have complete assurance that we are accepted by God and secure in his love? Because Christ took the penalty for our sin when he died on the cross. Paul wrote back in 3 v 25: "God presented Christ as a sacrifice of atonement, through the shedding of his blood—to be received by faith."

And what does God plan to do in my life? Romans 8 shows us that the glory of being a Christian does not lie merely in the fact that we are no longer estranged from God because of our rebellion. It is also recognizing who we are and who we have become through Christ that is genuinely thrilling.

To grow in our relationship to Christ doesn't mean we are signing up for some dreary self-improvement program—as we shall soon discover when we delve into Romans 8!

Historical Context

It is generally believed that the apostle Paul wrote this letter to Roman believers around AD56 from Corinth. The believers in Rome comprised of Gentile and Jewish Christians, and this book was written most likely during Paul's third missionary journey, as he was about to set out for Jerusalem (Romans 15 v 25). His plan was to visit Rome after Jerusalem, which is exactly what he did.

Since Paul had never been to Rome, he outlines the gospel so that his teaching will not be confused by what he calls "false teachers." Paul makes it clear that the apostles did not invent the gospel; it was revealed and entrusted to them by God. Before we come to chapter 8, Paul explains why the whole human race desperately needs the gospel, both Gentiles and Jews alike: "for all have sinned and fall short of the glory of God" (3 v 23). Beginning in chapter 3, Paul shows how the grace of God has been revealed through Christ and his gospel.

In this study we'll see Paul talking about the work of the Spirit. In 8 v 2-11 we learn that the Spirit gives us new hearts and makes us spiritually alive; he shows us our sin but also gives us assurance that it is forgiven and the power to defeat it. The Spirit will raise us to life just as he raised Jesus to new life.

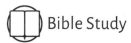

Bible Study

Read Romans 8 v 14-17

In pre-modern times people's identities and careers were fashioned by who their parents were and what level of society they were born into. Ironically, in our modern western age of individualism and rights, where we are free to choose our careers and even our identities, people seem to feel more insecure and alone than ever. We struggle to know who we are—or if we even belong.

1. Verse 14 describes people who are now trusting Jesus. What two things are true of them?

_____

_____

In the Greco-Roman culture of Paul's day, the term "adoption" had great significance. It meant that a child was deliberately chosen to continue the father's name and to inherit his estate. The adopted child was never considered inferior or less loved than his own children, conceived by him and his wife.

2. What is the difference between how a slave feels and how a son feels (v 15)? How might their actions and motivations be different?

_____

_____

_____

_____

o How has the Spirit replaced fear with freedom in your own walk with God?

_____

_____

_____

_____

3. Having received the "Spirit [which brings about our] adoption," how are we helped by the Spirit to know we are God's reconciled children (v 15b-16)?

_____

_____

_____

_____

The Aramaic term for father, "*Abba*," was the more intimate way that children addressed their earthly father. Jews would have never addressed God in this informal manner, yet Jesus did it and encouraged his followers to do so. Paul says that the Spirit prompts us in our prayers to call God "*Abba*," which means we address God as a small child speaking to their father.

The highest privilege of the Christian life is our adoption as children into God's eternal family through God's one and only Son, Jesus Christ. Verses 15b and 16 are a beautiful picture of the believer's joy and security that come from realizing that God has truly adopted us! We have been made full members of his family, and we receive all the privileges of belonging to God's family. We are loved and we belong. These are not only objective facts but the Spirit makes us inwardly *aware* that we are now God's own children.

o Think about what God is like. Why is it amazing that we can relate to God as our loving Father?

_____

_____

_____

_____

o How is this truth especially helpful for those who come from less than ideal families?

_____

_____

_____

_____

4. If we are God's children, then how else are we to think of ourselves (v 17a)? What do we inherit (v 17b)?

_____

_____

_____

_____

_____

5. As our Father, God gives us everything that belongs to his Son, Jesus—both the shape of his earthly life and the wonder of his eternal life. We gain both the sufferings and the glory (v 17b). How does this set our expectations for what the Christian life is like, and why is it always worth it?

_____

_____

_____

_____

o What are some ways that Christians today suffer for Christ? Have you suffered for Christ in any way?

_____

_____

_____

Paul proceeds to reflect (v 18-27) on how our present suffering is not worth comparing with the glory that will one day be revealed in us. Paul reminds us that in our trials and suffering God is at work through the Spirit, who helps us in our weakness (v 26), and who intercedes for us when we don't know how to pray (v 26-27).

Read Romans 8 v 28-29

6. What does verse 28 promise, and to whom? Why is this remarkable given that our lives include suffering, difficulty and disappointment?

_____

_____

_____

_____

_____

7. In what ways will God work towards our ultimate good—even in seemingly bad situations?

_____

_____

_____

_____

8. The word "predestined" means "decided beforehand." What has God decided to do in the life of every adopted child of his (v 29)? What does this mean?

_____

_____

_____

○ How does it help us to know what God thinks is "good" in verse 28?

_____

_____

_____

○ Think about what you know of Jesus. Why can we be confident that God's plan for our lives is wonderful? (Why is it wonderful that God will work to make us more and more like him?)

_____

_____

_____

_____

Live What You Learn

We have learned that all believers are filled with and led by the Spirit, have received the Spirit of adoption, and cry "*Abba*, Father" as the Spirit bears witness to them that they are children of God, and therefore his heirs. Indeed, Paul tells us "the Spirit himself testifies with our spirit that we are God's children" (v 16).

○ *Reflect on a hard time in your Christian life. How might God have been making you more like Jesus through this difficulty?*

○ *Are there areas in your life right now where you need to hang on to the promise in verse 28?*

 Following Jesus

○ *What, then, shall we say in response to these things? (v 31)*—to God's love for us and plan for us?

○ *If God is for us, who can be against us? (v 31)* No matter what happens, God has the last word—we need not fear.

○ *He who did not spare his own Son ... how will he not also ... give us all things? (v 32)* The cross is our guarantee of the faithful, loving generosity of God.

○ *Who will bring any charge against those whom God has chosen? (v 33)* Our case has already been decided. We are declared as accepted by God.

○ *Who then is the one who condemns? (v 34)* No one—because Jesus has died for our sins, taking all the condemnation that we deserve.

○ *Who shall separate us from the love of Christ? (v 35)* Just as Christ proved his love for us through his sufferings, so our sufferings cannot separate us from the love of Christ.

○ Nothing can thwart God's purpose for us or his commitment to us, because we are his beloved children.

 Life Stories

⬆ Praying Together

This would be a good time to share with each other where you would most appreciate prayer—maybe concerning things that have struck you in this passage.

- ○ Ask God to help you more deeply internalize the truths you have read—like experiencing the fact that you are a son or daughter of God.

- ○ Perhaps you could share what is blocking you from experiencing God's love and assurance, and ask God to remove or heal whatever is giving you difficulty.

- ○ Thank God for his promise that you are his child. Ask God for the faith to believe that what he says is true.

Remember, our prayers don't need to be long or complex; a single heartfelt sentence will do! God looks at the heart, not at a picture-perfect prayer.

You'll find some more books about the themes of this session on page 61.

⬇ Going Deeper: The Primacy Of Love

If you wish to explore the topic we are studying in greater depth, then read this section at home. If you have any questions about it, feel free to pursue your questions with your group's leader.

It is an amazing thought that the same Spirit who raised Jesus from the dead comes and lives in us from the moment we first believe in Jesus! "That power is the same as the mighty strength he exerted when he raised Christ from the dead" (Ephesians 1 v 19-20). We now have the outworking of Jesus' own life and power through his Spirit dwelling within us.

When we become Christians, God's Spirit gives us a new power, new relationships, new obligations and new gifts. But none of these are what matter most. It is not gifts or power or experiences that we should most seek.

The twentieth-century pastor Dr. Martyn Lloyd-Jones wrote: "We should always be seeking the Lord Jesus Christ himself, to know him, and know his love and be witnesses for him and to minister to his glory." In other words: *We must put 1 Corinthians 13 at the centre.* In that chapter, Paul promises to "show you the most excellent way" to live (1 Corinthians 12 v 31).

Read 1 Corinthians 13 v 1-13

1. What are the spiritual gifts that Paul mentions in verses 1-3?

_____

o What are they worth if they're not accompanied by love?

_____

2. What seems to be God's purpose in how we exercise the gifts he gives us?

_____

3. As we think about the gifts God has given us, how might it be tempting to use them in wrong ways or with wrong motivations?

_____

_____

Having described the importance of love, Paul now goes on in verses 4-8 to define love. It quickly becomes obvious that the love being described in these verses has its source in God and his gift of Christ. Just as Christ lived and died for others—supremely in the cross—the way of love is most truly seen in having a Christ-like concern, respect and regard for the welfare of others above our own interests or needs.

4. Paul gives 15 separate pictures of what love looks like! List some of them.

_____

_____

o What characteristics of love are present in your life? What characteristics do you find hardest to display?

_____

_____

_____

5. Jesus said that all the world will know that we are his disciples by the love that we have for one another (see John 13 v 34-35). What do you think is the end result of a life lived without the love of God? And of a life with the love of God?

_____

_____

6. What are the things that will cease once we are in heaven (1 Corinthians 13 v 8)?

_____

o Why is this the case (v 9-12)?

_____

_____

7. What will last eternally (v 13)?

_____

8. How does verse 12 excite you about what a Christian's eternity will be like?

_____

_____

9. Paul writes: "Now these three remain: faith, hope and love. But the greatest of these is love" (v 13). How has this passage shown why this is so?

_____

_____

_____

2. Growing Together In Christ

Acts 2 v 36-47 and Ephesians 4 v 1-6

Picture this scene. It's the Last Supper, on the night before Jesus dies. Jesus tells his disciples as they gather to eat: "I am going away" (John 14 v 28). They are deeply distressed and full of fear at the thought of facing life without him. But what Jesus says next perplexes them even more: "It is for your good that I am going away" (16 v 7).

How could it possibly be to the disciples' advantage to live without Jesus' physical presence?! Jesus continues: "Unless I go away, the Advocate [the Holy Spirit] will not come to you; but if I go, I will send him to you" (v 7). When Jesus was here on earth, he was limited by space and time. It was his physical departure and return to heaven that made possible the coming of the Holy Spirit. Now there would be no barriers of space and time to prevent the disciples—or future believers like us!—from being in intimate contact with Christ, through his Spirit.

And so when the crucified, risen Jesus was about to ascend into heaven, his final words were terribly important: "Do not leave Jerusalem, but wait for the gift my Father promised" (Acts 1 v 4).

So his followers returned to Jerusalem, where they prayed and waited for Christ to send the promised Holy Spirit. Ten days later, the Spirit came in power. That day is referred to as Pentecost—and, as we'll see, that day is also the day the church was born.

 Historical Context

In Acts 2 we read the exciting account of the Spirit's descent onto the first followers of Jesus. Just as Jesus had promised, when the Holy Spirit came upon them they received divine power—which included being empowered to proclaim Jesus boldly. Only weeks earlier, Peter had lied about even knowing Christ! Now he was boldly and publicly preaching the good news to a large crowd in Jerusalem, some of whom would have likely overseen Jesus' crucifixion (v 23, 36)!

What did the experience at Pentecost have to do with the birth of the New Testament church? The Holy Spirit used Peter's speech to draw many to faith in Jesus. Acts 2 v 41 tells us that while the first followers of Jesus had numbered about 120, after Peter's sermon over 3,000 others joined the community of faith! What did they do as a result of their conversion? They joyfully went to church! It is the work of the Spirit, not only to transform us into Christ's image, but to build up the church.

In Acts 2 v 5 we read: "Now there were staying in Jerusalem God-fearing Jews from every nation under heaven." When the Holy Spirit came and filled the believers with his presence, he also supernaturally enabled them to speak in various languages so they could communicate the gospel to one and all. The crowd outside heard the commotion and rushed to see what was happening: "Amazed and perplexed, they asked one another, 'What does this mean?'" (2 v 12). Peter then responded with a powerful sermon. Our reading picks up part-way through Peter's speech, as recorded for us in the book of Acts.

 Bible Study

Read Acts 2 v 36-47

1. When we are ready to place our trust in Jesus, what should we do, and what is God's promised response (v 38)?

_____

_____

_____

2. Why do you think Peter lists the public act of baptism as part of our faith response?

_____

_____

_____

Baptism is an outward sign that we now belong to Jesus' community. It is a public sign of our decision to be followers of Christ, signifying that we believe in Jesus as the risen Lord, we have repented of our sins, and we have received his Holy Spirit. Baptism itself does not bring about these spiritual realities— rather, it reflects what has already taken place in our lives. If we have never been baptised, then this is an important and glorious thing to do.

3. Luke (the writer of Acts) tells us that the early church devoted themselves to the apostles' teaching (v 42). "Apostle" was a title given to each of Jesus' original disciples, who had been with him for all of his public ministry on earth. Why do you think the new Christians were so keen to hear what the apostles had to say?

_____

_____

_____

4. How did God give extra proof that the apostles' teaching was true (v 43)?

_____

5. Why is teaching and learning from the Old Testament and New Testament such a key part of healthy church life and Christian maturity today (see John 16 v 12-15 and 2 Timothy 3 v 15-17)?

_____

_____

_____

The apostles' teaching has now come to us in the form of the New Testament. The Old Testament pointed forward to the coming of Jesus and the salvation he would achieve. The authors of the Bible were inspired or "carried along" by the Holy Spirit so that they recorded what God wanted to say (2 Peter 1 v 21). Today as we read the Bible, the same Spirit illuminates our minds and hearts to hear the Father speak about his Son, his salvation and how we should live in response to him (1 Corinthians 2 v 12).

6. When we come to know Christ, we are brought into a fellowship with other believers. His Spirit gives us a love for other Christians that we never had before. Initially we may feel we have little in common, yet because of our mutual love for the Lord Jesus, we discover that we share the most important bond of all. This compassion and love isn't only on the emotional level; it is also practical, as pictured in Acts 2 v 44-45.

What do you think happened in these new believers' hearts to free them to be so generous with their physical possessions?

_____

_____

_____

This sharing of property and possessions among the early Christians was voluntary. Verse 46 tells us that they broke bread in their homes. Evidently many members of the early church still had homes, so the implication is that the selling and giving of possessions (v 45) were as circumstances required them, not once and for all. As the early Christians saw others in need, it seems they sought to supply those needs from their own resources.

7. Acts tells us that early Christian prayer and worship of Jesus took place both formally (in the temple courts) and informally (in people's homes). Why do you think the early Christians gathered in both of these ways?

_____

_____

_____

_____

The description particularly mentions prayer and "the breaking of bread." The second refers to what we commonly call "Communion" or the "Eucharist" or the "Lord's supper." It usually involves eating a piece of bread in remembrance of Jesus' broken body and drinking a sip of red wine, which Jesus likened to his blood being poured out for the forgiveness of our sins (Matthew 26 v 27-29). Taking communion is when we reflect on all that Jesus has done for us and we receive afresh his life into our lives. But it is also what we look forward to doing when we eat and drink with him in eternity!

8. The gathering of the early church was evidently a joyful occasion! What do you think made them so full of joy? Luke also tells us that when the people gathered, they spent time "praising God" (Acts 2 v 47). How might we grow in our praise of and thankfulness to God?

_____

_____

_____

_____

_____

o How does verse 47 show us that the early church was not self-absorbed?

_____

_____

_____

The picture of the church in Acts 2 paints for us a beautiful picture of God's design for church life.

Yet churches continually fall short of this ideal in various ways. That should not be a surprise to us; after all, while Christians are forgiven and are being transformed into the likeness of Christ, we are all still "works-in-progress."

God's design for his people is for them to join together in local church life. In this second passage, the apostle Paul teaches how imperfect Christians are to relate to other imperfect Christians.

9. Paul gives four instructions in verse 2. Paul evidently thought that church life wouldn't always be easy. How do these verses demonstrate that?

_____

_____

10. What do Christians have in common, despite all their differences (v 4-6)?

_____

_____

_____

Verses 4-6 point to God's trinitarian nature—referring to the Spirit, the Lord (ie: the Lord Jesus) and God the Father. Just as God has one essence that is shared by three divine Persons from eternity, so God's design for his people is for them to be a community—a community that is diverse, and yet bonded together in unity and love. When Paul says in Ephesians 4 v 3 that we are to "make every effort to keep the unity of the Spirit through the bond of peace," it is clear that while it won't always be easy to love people who are different from us, it pleases God and is worth the effort.

$\rightarrow$ Live What You Learn

Being a Christian isn't merely learning how to grow your individual faith. The Bible stresses the importance of belonging to a community of faith who are committed in their connection to God and Christ, and in their relationships with one another. This is clear in Jesus' command in John 15 v 12: "My command is this: love each other as I have loved you." When we become Christians, we become part of a new community of love—the church. This means that church isn't an optional extra. By becoming a Christian, we have become part of the worldwide church, and we express that by being part of a local church.

o *In Acts 2 v 42 we are told that the new believers were devoted to the church. How does their attitude toward the church compare to your own?*

o *What do you find difficult or exciting about church?*

Following Jesus: Who Is The Holy Spirit?

- The coming of the Spirit means Jesus' followers have God's presence and power within them.

- The Holy Spirit is a person—fully God, a member of the Trinity. His mission is to reveal to us who Jesus is.

- We need to "keep in step with the Spirit" (Galatians 5 v 25). We do this by:

  1. REMEMBERING Jesus is with us by his Spirit.

  2. REJOICING and thanking God that we have access to his power and wisdom.

  3. REQUESTING the Spirit's help when we need it through the day.

  4. RENEWING our commitment to keep in step with the Spirit by opposing our inclination to fall back into self-reliance and self-rule.

- These are habits we have to work at, from the moment we wake each morning.

 ## Life Stories

 ## Praying Together

- Thank God for his gifts of the Holy Spirit and the church, which help us to know him better.

- Ask God to help you remember that his Spirit is within you. Tell him that you want to walk in step with the Spirit.

- Ask God to help you find a church where the Bible is preached faithfully and where you feel at home.

- Memorize this verse, where Christ assured Paul: "My grace is sufficient for you, for my power is made perfect in weakness" (2 Corinthians 12 v 9).

You'll find some more books about the themes of this session on page 61.

 Going Deeper: Making Church Part Of Our Life

Going to church

Going to a new place and meeting new people can be daunting. But it's much easier if you go along with someone else. Ask a Christian friend whether they could go along with you. Most Christians understand that it's scary to go to church for the first time—you won't be frowned upon if you're not exactly sure what's going on!

What happens in a church on Sunday?

The exact blend of what happens differs from church to church. But there are various core components you can expect. There will be a time when people pray to their heavenly Father about their concerns. People will sing together in praise to God, thanking him for all he is and what he has done for us. Singing is a great way of applying amazing truths about Jesus to our hearts. There will be teaching from the Bible. Fairly regularly, though not necessarily in every service, the Lord's Supper—bread and wine—will be shared. There's often time to chat afterwards to get to know Christians of different ages and backgrounds. If you have further questions about what church is like, ask a Christian friend.

Why are there so many types of churches?

Jesus only ever talked of "my church," in the singular. Jesus' church is composed of all those who love, follow and trust him. Many of the distinctions between churches have more to do with culture than belief. Even though they differ in style, churches that are biblically faithful love and worship the same God, and so are part of the one universal church, of which Jesus is head.

Different denominations of church emerge when churches split over disagreements. Sometimes these are over important questions of belief. Sadly, at other times these splits are over much more trivial issues. A key thing to remember is that the style of a Sunday service is much less important than its content and focus. The essential thing is to find a church which looks to the Bible as the primary way of knowing God, and which places lots of emphasis on the finished work of Jesus at the cross as our means of forgiveness.

Why isn't it enough to meet with my friends now and then or listen to worship music or walk in nature?

We've seen that God's design is for diverse Christians to come together to help each other grow. Because church is family, you'll meet and learn from Christians of different ages and backgrounds. Different sorts of people need each other and can serve each other differently.

A good church is committed to teaching parts of the Bible and important subjects that you probably wouldn't study if you only meet every now and then with friends or rely only on worship albums. The church is also committed to the longer-term spiritual growth of its members. But it isn't simply about what we can receive. God also asks us to give and serve fellow believers in the context of the church community; and it's impossible to do that if you're not part of a local church!

How might I get involved in a local church?

Remember what church is all about: growing together in love for Jesus and seeking to serve one another as we can. Part of being involved in church is going regularly—even by your regular presence you'll encourage other members of the church. Additionally, seeking to tell your story and sharing encouragements about how God is at work in your life will give other Christians extra reasons to be thankful to God.

There might also be practical ways in which you can serve at a local church. As you go along regularly to a church, you'll discover that God has taken you to that particular local church and given you particular gifts (of talents, or time, and so on) that you can contribute to that church. So be looking for opportunities to serve the rest of the church. If there aren't obvious ways to serve, then ask one of the leaders where they need more volunteers. Ideally we can find opportunities to serve that fit the gifts God has given us. But don't only consider the more public ways to serve, like welcoming or leading or playing music. It is also good to think about the unseen things... like putting the Bibles out before people get there, washing up the tea cups, baby-sitting so a family can get out to a Bible study, or cooking a meal for someone who is ill.

3. Why Pray When We Can Worry Instead?

Matthew 6 v 5-15

What does the Spirit use to enable us to become more like Jesus? One way is through Bible study and prayer. Reading God's word and praying will draw us closer to Jesus, transform us into his likeness and help us understand the will of our Father.

Prayer is the most human act we can engage in. When we pray, we are speaking in our mother tongue, because God created us for intimate relationship with him. We are never more human, never more ourselves, than when we pray.

Why should we pray? Left to ourselves we can easily become selfish and preoccupied, but prayer refocuses our attention on God. Prayer shifts our preoccupation away from ourselves and toward God—toward the God who loves us, who is waiting to hear from us and who wants us to know his will and his ways.

But *how* should we pray? Anything that smacks of techniques or formulas is out of place, because God wants us to relate to him and love him as a Person, as our Father. So we need to come into God's presence and communicate in a way that is reverent but real.

So then, *what* should we pray? Do we have guidelines that help us know what to say? Are there particular things that the King of the universe wants us to talk to him about? That is what we are about to explore in Matthew's Gospel, as we look at the most famous prayer of all.

Historical Context

In chapter 6 v 1-8 of Matthew's Gospel, Jesus taught the disciples that our devotion to God must be sincere. We are not to parade our devotion in order to impress others with our piety. When we pray, for example, it is not in order to impress others with how spiritual we are. Nor, Jesus said, do we need to use lots of words in order to get God's attention. God already knows what our needs are. We pray not to inform God on matters in which he is ignorant, but to worship him and to open our hearts and lives to him.

Jesus taught the disciples a prayer that we now refer to as the "Lord's Prayer." This prayer is widely considered to be a pattern for prayer—a map to guide us as we pray. This doesn't mean there is nothing else we can pray about—nor is this the only model of prayer offered in the Bible. But it is an excellent place to start.

Bible Study

Read Matthew 6 v 5-15

1. How does Jesus teach us to focus our prayers first on God and his priorities, before we focus on our own needs?

The Bible teaches that while our feelings truly matter to God, they don't come first. When we take a slow, calm, reassuring gaze at God, and remember his greatness, as well as his love and patience, it not only calms our spirits but our faith is deepened in the process.

2. How does Jesus tell us to address our Creator God?

○ How does the knowledge that God is our loving Father change our feelings about prayer and even how we talk to God as we pray?

_____

_____

We saw in Study 1 the tremendous security of knowing that we have been adopted by God. Even if our earthly experience of a father has been difficult and painful, God is still our perfect Father. For Jesus to call God "Father" means that God is a Person, not merely a "Higher Power" or a "Blind Force." God wants to know what we have to say. He is loving, not aloof. Therefore, our childlike trust in going to our loving heavenly Father is the foundation of all effective prayer.

J.I. Packer wrote: "If you want to judge how well a person understands Christianity, find out how much he makes of the thought of being God's child, and having God as his Father. If this is not the thought that prompts and controls his worship and prayers and his whole outlook on life, it means that he does not understand Christianity very well at all." (*Knowing God*, p 201).

3. Why is it helpful to remember that God is not only our Father, but the supreme King of heaven?

_____

_____

_____

4. When Jesus says: "Hallowed be your name," he is referring to God's essence: in particular his holiness—but also his power, justice, mercy, truth and love. When Jesus asks that God's name be hallowed, he is saying: *May God's name be known and respected on all the earth*.

What are ways that God's character can become more evident in our lives so that others may see who God truly is? (In our speech? worship? lifestyle?)

_____

_____

_____

Describing how we can hallow God's name, the late author Ray Stedman wrote: "May the whole of my life be a source of delight to You and may it be an honor to the name which I bear, which is Your name."

5. When Jesus tells us in verse 10 to pray: "Your kingdom come, your will be done, on earth as it is in heaven," we are reminded that God's kingdom already reigns in heaven. But one day God's kingdom will reign on earth, when Christ returns at the end of history.

   Besides praying for Christ's return, in what ways can we pray for God's kingdom to come more and more fully on earth?

   _____

   _____

   _____

6. Until now the petitions have focused on praising God and the great causes of God's kingdom. Now Jesus' attention turns to the personal needs of his followers. After listing three items of prayer for God's glory, Jesus now balances them with three petitions for our needs.

   By asking God to help us in our daily needs, such as food, what does Jesus tell us about God's nature and our nature (v 11)?

   _____

   _____

7. What ongoing need as Christians does verse 12 remind us of?

   _____

   _____

o Why is it humbling that we have to ask for this, yet reassuring that Jesus tells us that we can?

   _____

   _____

When we sin, it doesn't mean we cease to be children of God—but sin prevents us from having the closeness, peace and joy that we experience when we are walking in obedience to God. We must never forget that confession of sin is one of God's great gifts to us!

8. How does God's daily forgiveness of our sins help us to extend forgiveness to others?

_____

_____

_____

○ If we refuse to forgive another, what might it suggest that we haven't appreciated about the gospel message?

_____

_____

_____

"Someone once said it was a brilliant stroke when Jesus took the one thing we need most and want most of all from God—forgiveness—and tied it to the one thing we are, by nature, most reluctant to do—forgive those who injure us. " (Peter Lewis, *The Lord's Prayer*)

9. Next Jesus prepares us for the tests and temptations of life. While God may allow his children to pass through times of testing, the Bible makes it clear that God tempts no one to do evil (James 1 v 13). However, given our fallen world and natures, it is inevitable that temptations will arise.

Because we have weaknesses and vulnerabilities, what does Jesus encourage us to pray ahead of time (Matthew 6 v 13)?

_____

_____

o What practical things can we do to avoid temptation?

_____

_____

_____

1 Corinthians 10 v 13 tells us that God always answers our prayer one way or another: either by enabling us to avoid temptation, or by giving us a way out of temptation: "No temptation has overtaken you except what is common to mankind. And God is faithful; he will not let you be tempted beyond what you can bear." When we realize we are being tempted, we need first to pray and then look for how God is providing a way out.

10. When we recognize that we are in a vulnerable situation (be it demonic temptation or "evil" in a more general sense), what does Jesus tell us to pray (Matthew 6 v 13b)?

_____

_____

o How have you experienced God's help and deliverance in times of temptation or evil?

_____

_____

_____

_____

(→) Live What You Learn

In Jesus' concluding remarks on prayer (v 14-15), he makes clear what he expects of his people. Forgiveness is a vital characteristic of God's people. Jesus assures us of the certainty that as we forgive others, God also forgives us. It isn't about returning the compliment; rather, our willingness to forgive gives evidence that the grace of God is at work in our lives.

- How does reflecting on God's forgiveness for us provide us with the emotional resolve and resources to forgive those who have badly hurt us?

- Is there someone God is asking you to forgive? What is a first step you could take to forgive this person?

- When you consider your own prayer life, how has the Lord's Prayer encouraged or challenged you?

 ## Following Jesus: Learning How To Pray With Hannah

- Hannah's story is found in 1 Samuel 1 v 1 – 2 v 11.

- Hannah's prayer was reverent but real.

- Her prayer reveals a biblical way of dealing with our emotions: not denying our feelings or being dominated by them, but *praying* our feelings.

- Her prayer reveals that authentic prayer changes us: she thought she most needed a child, but realized she most needed God.

- Hannah was guided by God's word, not her own emotions: she believed she would become pregnant before she was pregnant.

- We can pray boldly, because the God of creation cares for our individual needs.

 ## Life Stories

 ## Praying Together

- Thank God that we can pray boldly. Thank him that he cares about our individual needs and emotions.

- Look back at question 5 and ask for God's kingdom to come more and more fully on earth in the ways you wrote down.

o Ask God to meet your daily needs.

o Spend time thanking God for the forgiveness he has shown to you in Christ, and ask him to help you forgive others.

o Perhaps you could share with the group some specific areas of temptation or evil you're facing at the moment, and then pray for one another.

You'll find some more books about the themes of this session on page 61.

 # Going Deeper: Bible Overview

The Bible can seem a very intimidating book. With 66 different books within its covers, covering a few thousand years of history, and focused almost exclusively on a small chunk of land on the eastern Mediterranean coast, it's not an easy book to start to read and understand, let alone see what it means for your life!

What makes it a whole lot easier is to realize that there is a central thread that runs throughout it. It is 66 books with one story and one central theme. There are many ways to summarize that theme, but here is one: "We tell you the good news: what God promised our ancestors he has fulfilled for us, their children, by raising up Jesus" (Acts 13 v 32-33).

In this single sentence, the apostle Paul summed up the story of the whole Bible! God is a promise-making God. Throughout history, he has made extravagant, wonderful promises to humanity. And, crucially, God is also a promise-fulfilling God. What he says, he does. And Paul is telling us that he has fulfilled all his promises in the life, death, resurrection and rule of one human—Jesus. Here is how this great story of God making and keeping promises unfolds through the Bible. See it as a nine-act play...

1. Creation

Bible section: Genesis 1 – 2

Main characters: The first man and woman.

What happened: God created everything and made people to know him, enjoy him, and enjoy living under his rule and looking after his world.

The promise: A very good world to live in.

2. The fall

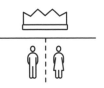

Bible section: Genesis 3 – 11

Main characters: Adam and Eve; Cain and Abel; Noah.

What happened: Tempted by the devil, the first humans decided not to live under God's rule, but to grasp at rule for themselves. God's judgment was to shut them out from his presence, give them imperfect relationships with each other, and make them live in an imperfect world, facing death.

The promise: God promised that a baby would be born who would crush the devil and reverse the effect of the fall. We are looking for a human who can defeat the devil.

3. God's covenant

Bible section: Genesis 12 – 50

Main characters: Abraham and Sarah, Isaac and Rebekah, Jacob (renamed Israel) and Esau, Leah and Rachel, Joseph and his brothers.

What happened: God told Abraham to leave his homeland and go to a land which God would give him. Abraham obeyed, and reached the land. But by the time of Abraham's great-grandchildren, Joseph and his brothers, his family were living out of the land, in Egypt.

The promise: God promised that from Abraham he would make a people, living in his land, under his rule and blessing—and that through one of Abraham's descendants, he would bless people throughout the world. We are looking for a human descended from Abraham who can bring blessing.

4. The exodus

Bible section: Exodus, Leviticus, Numbers, Deuteronomy

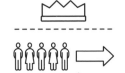

Main characters: Moses, Pharaoh, Miriam, Aaron, Balaam, Joshua, Caleb.

What happened: God rescued his people, who were in slavery in Egypt. He judged all people, but told his people that instead of their firstborn sons dying, a lamb could die in their place. God brought his people out of Egypt and took them to the verge of the land he'd promised Abraham.

The promise: God would rescue his people from the ultimate judgment of death by providing a lamb to die in their place, taking their judgment.

5. The early monarchy

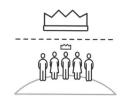

Bible section: Joshua, Judges, Ruth, 1&2 Samuel, 1 Chronicles, 2 Chronicles 1 – 9, 1 Kings 1 – 11, Psalms, Proverbs, Ecclesiastes, Song of Songs.

Main characters: Joshua, the judges (including Deborah, Gideon and Samson), Ruth, Eli, Samuel, Saul, David, Bathsheba, Solomon.

What happened: God's people did not live his way in his land; so he provided kings to rule them, leading them in obedience to him and defeating their enemies so they could enjoy life in his land. David was the greatest of these kings; but he died, and after him the kings were more and more flawed.

The promise: God would provide a king descended from David who would not die, but would rule his people perfectly for ever. We are looking for a human from David's family who can rule perfectly.

6. The prophets

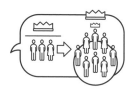

Bible section: 2 Chronicles 10 – 36, 1 Kings 12 – 22, Ezra, Nehemiah, Esther, Psalms, Isaiah, Jeremiah, Lamentations, Ezekiel, Daniel, Hosea, Joel, Amos, Obadiah, Jonah, Micah, Nahum, Habakkuk, Zephaniah, Haggai, Zechariah, Malachi.

Main characters: Elijah, Elisha, Ahab and Jezebel, Hezekiah, Josiah, Nebuchadnezzar, all the prophets listed above!

What happened: Led by bad kings, the people kept ignoring God and his laws. So God sent them prophets, who warned them that judgment would come but that salvation would then follow. Eventually, God's people were exiled from the land, and though they returned, they found that they did not enjoy much peace or prosperity. The Old Testament finishes with them still waiting for God's promises to be fulfilled.

The promise: God would judge his people, but he would also save them, giving them a future beyond the judgment much greater than anything they had seen before.

7. Jesus of Nazareth

Bible section: Matthew, Mark, Luke, John ("the Gospels")

Main characters: Joseph and Mary, King Herod, John the Baptist, Jesus of Nazareth, the disciples, Pontius Pilate.

What happened: Jesus taught about God, claimed to be the Son of God and proved it through his miracles. He attracted, and then lost, a huge following. When he entered the capital, Jerusalem, he aroused the envy and anger of the religious establishment, who arrested him and had him executed on a cross. Three days later, he rose to life.

The fulfillment: Jesus' resurrection is the great proof that he is the fulfiller of all God's promises. He calls people to live under his loving rule, brings God's blessing to those who follow him, has defeated the devil, death and sin, and has died to take God's judgment so that he can offer a perfect future to his people.

8. Mission

Bible section: Acts, Romans, 1 Corinthians, 2 Corinthians, Galatians, Ephesians, Philippians, Colossians, 1 Thessalonians, 2 Thessalonians, 1 Timothy, 2 Timothy, Titus, Philemon, Hebrews, James, 1 Peter, 2 Peter, 1 John, 2 John, 3 John, Jude, Revelation 1–19

Main characters: The apostles (particularly Peter, Paul, James and John), the early church (particularly Stephen and Philip), the first church leaders (especially Timothy and Titus).

What happened: Jesus ascended to heaven and sent the Holy Spirit to empower his people to tell the truth about him. Gatherings ("churches") spread from Jerusalem to Rome and beyond. This period of history includes today: God's people are still devoting themselves to each other and telling the world about his Son.

The fulfillment: The blessing promised to Abraham, and offered through Jesus, is coming to people from all around the world.

9. The new creation

Bible section: Revelation 20 – 22

Main character: Jesus Christ

What will happen: Jesus will return, and judge and punish all that is wrong with the world, including sin, death and the devil. He will recreate the world perfectly.

The fulfillment: God's people will live under God's King in God's perfect, eternal kingdom.

With this framework in mind, wherever you are in the Bible you can have some idea of roughly what is going on. You can read a passage and ask yourself:

○ *Which of the nine acts am I in here?*

○ *Is God making a promise in this section of the Bible?*

○ *Is God fulfilling a promise partially (in the Old Testament) or fully (in the New Testament)?*

○ *How is this passage encouraging me to love and trust Jesus more, as the fulfiller of all God's promises?*

It will take more than a lifetime to grasp all the intricacies and insights of what God has written through human authors. That's exciting! But this promise-fulfillment summary will get you started, or re-started, on that exciting journey. Why not start today?

4. Walking In Obedience

Ephesians 4 v 17 – 5 v 2

We can be secure and settled in our faith because, since we are children of God, God now lives in us by his Spirit. And God is transforming us into the image of his Son, Jesus, through means including his church, the Bible and prayer.

Frederick Nietzsche, the atheist German philosopher, once declared: "I might believe in the Redeemer if his followers looked more redeemed." This is a painful rebuke and it causes us to ask: *As Christians, are we actually any different to those around us? Are we actually becoming more like Jesus? And what will empower that kind of change?*

As we grow in faith, we may find ourselves taken aback that sin hasn't been eliminated from our lives. If anything, we seem to be *more* aware of sin's pull! But this only proves what God has done: because we have the Holy Spirit's presence in our lives, we are now more sensitive to what displeases God. The fact that we feel a "pull" between what our old sinful nature wants and what the Holy Spirit wants is proof that the Spirit lives in us and that we belong to Jesus!

We can be confident that this new life is made possible because of Jesus' death on the cross which dealt with "the old," while his Spirit living in us is bringing about "the new." But this change also involves our willingness to turn from sin. However, we must be patient. There is no such thing as instant godliness. It's a lifelong process. And in this session, we're looking at what it means to walk in obedience and grow in obedience.

 Historical Context

The apostle Paul wrote his letter to Christians in Ephesus (in present-day Turkey) to encourage Gentile converts in their Christian faith. They were brought up in a pagan way of life; that had to now be abandoned. But Paul wanted them to appreciate the dignity of their calling, and to understand its implications not only for their heavenly destiny, but also for how they must live lives worthy of the gospel of Jesus Christ in this world.

How do we co-operate with the Spirit in bringing about our transformation? There are many ways in which the Bible refers to this process of transformation. Sometimes, as in the passage we are about to read, we are told to "put on" the new and "put off" the old. Becoming Christ-like is a process of change where the old way of life is replaced with the new.

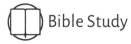 Bible Study

Read Ephesians 4 v 17 – 5 v 2

The concept of sin in the Bible may surprise us. We tend to think of sin as individual acts of behavioral wrongdoing. But the Bible points to what lies *behind* these behaviors. Jesus locates the source of the human problem in the heart—at the very core of our being (Mark 7 v 20-23).

Paul likewise places emphasis on the heart. In our politically correct world we may find Paul's refusal to mince words a bit shocking. But Paul, like a spiritual surgeon, refuses to settle for superficial behavior change. He knows that without going to the root of the problem—the heart—we will not be able to grasp the enormity of what Christ has done for us. Nor will we understand how gloriously different our lives are meant to be.

In this section, Paul paints a vivid picture of contrasts, between the way we once lived and the way of living now available to us. He wants us to see that we are to live a life that stands out in bold relief from the culture around us.

1. Paul states that people are separated from the life of God because of the hardening of their hearts (Ephesians 4 v 18). What do you think he means by this phrase?

_____

2. What does a hardened heart lead to?

_____

_____

Ignorance here doesn't mean a lack of intelligence or knowledge—it means ignoring the life that God generously offers; an attitude that prefers blindness to seeing and loving God.

3. In verse 19 Paul states that hardness of heart affects our behavior. Why do you think that life without God leads to a continual lust for more? What does sin promise but never do?

_____

_____

Paul now dramatically switches gears. He has given us a graphic picture of life before Christ so that we may see the dramatic contrast of our new life with the old one.

4. In verses 20-24, Paul describes the new life the Ephesians now have in Christ. Paul seems to be saying: _Be what you are! Be in practice what the calling of God has made you!_
   How does Paul contrast the old life with the new life in verses 22-24?

_____

_____

5. Paul speaks, in verse 23, about the importance of the mind in living a transformed life. This inward renewal is the work of the Holy Spirit, who progressively transforms us into the image of Christ. But we must participate with the Spirit.
   What practical things can we do to fill our minds with the beauty of God's truth?

_____

_____

o Why is meditating upon the beauty of Jesus, his love for us and his glorious purpose for our lives so effective in defeating sin (see Romans 12 v 2 or Philippians 4 v 8)?

_____

_____

_____

Paul seems to be saying that when we focus on God's goodness and desires for us, it causes us to delight in God. And delighting in God is a powerful remedy for defeating sin!

However, we need the same renewal of our mind in the way we see sin. The deception of sin lies in its short-term pleasure. Sin promises so much and delivers so little—afterwards leaving us feeling empty, ashamed and defeated. Sin is not our friend—it is utterly destructive.

6. What else does Paul tell us to do (Ephesians 4 v 24)? What is exciting about how he describes the new life here?

_____

_____

_____

o How does this help us deal with the objection that Christianity is just a list of don'ts?

_____

_____

_____

In verses 25-32, Paul describes what it looks like to take off the old self and put on the new self. But this is not a moral self-improvement course. We don't just sign up and work hard to change ourselves. Christianity isn't simply following a list of do's and don'ts. That would suggest that we can resist temptation and become the people God wants us to be through willpower alone. Paul reminds us that we have a new power within us. God's Spirit not only gives us new attitudes and desires but he will help us "put on" the new self we are becoming. Paul now gives some specific advice on the godly life we are to live.

7. Read verses 25-32. What exactly is the Christian to put off and put on?

_____

_____

_____

_____

_____

8. Note Paul's reasoning for each change of behaviour. Why is this reasoning important?

_____

_____

o For example, why is seething anger not only dangerous, but potentially destructive (v 26-27)? Why does Paul set a time limit on anger, do you think?

_____

_____

_____

9. In verses 4 v 32 – 5 v 1-2, Paul gives reasons for Christian obedience. What are these reasons and why is remembering them so important?

_____

_____

_____

Live What You Learn

God's desire is for the world to see the love of Jesus reflected in our lives and in our relationships. Because of what Christ has done for us, we are to demonstrate sacrificial love for others just as Christ sacrificed everything for us. We are called to be tender-hearted to the distresses and sufferings of others, kind, compassionate and forgiving.

o *What have we learned about being transformed into the image of Christ? How can we put Paul's principles of renewing our minds and practicing the principle of replacement into our lives?*

Think of a "new-self" action from these verses that you particularly struggle with.

o *When you act in an "old-self" way in that area, how is sin deceiving you?*

o *What are you forgetting about the gospel and your new identity as a child of God?*

o *What would change in your actions if you recognized sin's deceit and remembered the gospel at that moment?*

Following Jesus: The Process Of Repentance

o "If we confess our sins, he is faithful and just and will forgive us our sins and purify us from all unrighteousness" (1 John 1 v 9).

o Repentance is not the same as remorse or resolution. It is owning our sin, asking for forgiveness, and turning decisively away from it.

o The process of repentance is as follows:

　1. Name the name of the sin (the heart sin as well as the outward sin).

　2. Allow yourself to feel sorrow.

　3. Confess the sin to God, ask for forgiveness, and know that you are forgiven because Jesus died on the cross (even if you don't feel it).

　4. Ask God to strengthen you to change your behaviors or habits. Be accountable to another Christian.

 Life Stories

↑ Praying Together

o Ask God to help you to love him more than anything else, and to replace your current struggle against sin with a deeper love for and delight in him.

o Thank Jesus for going to the cross on your behalf. Confess any present sin, asking God's forgiveness and help to defeat it now and forever.

o Ask Jesus to help you see the person he wants you to be.

o Thank him for his promise to forgive and forget when you come to him in sincere repentance.

You'll find some more books about the themes of this session on page 62.

↓ Going Deeper: Spiritual Opposition & Temptation

Living for Jesus is glorious, but it is also challenging. We rejoice that we have been given new resources as believers: God's word and the power of the Holy Spirit. But also it doesn't take long to find that as Christians, we face opposition. First, there still exists within us our old nature, which seeks to draw us away from following Christ faithfully.

Second, we live in a world that tempts us because its values are so often contrary to the values of Christ and his kingdom. Lastly, the Bible teaches that we have an unseen enemy who seeks to undermine our faith in Christ and our obedience to him. He is called "the evil one" (Matthew 6 v 13), "the accuser" (Revelation 12 v 10), Satan (meaning adversary) and the devil (meaning slanderer).

As you read the Gospels, you find people being affected by evil spirits that are part of Satan's forces, which oppose Christ and his people. The apostle Paul writes: "For our struggle is not against flesh and blood, but against the rulers, against the authorities, against the powers of this dark world and against the spiritual forces of evil in the heavenly realms" (Ephesians 6 v 12).

This all may seem strange, unsettling, perhaps even medieval. How are we to understand these things the Bible clearly teaches? C.S. Lewis gives us very helpful wisdom when, in the preface to *The Screwtape Letters*, he warns against two mistaken responses to evil forces: "One is to disbelieve in their existence. The other is to believe, and to feel an excessive and unhealthy interest in them."

Satan's strategies

Temptation: Satan, for example, tempted Jesus, trying to get him to disobey his Father. He tempted Adam and Eve at the beginning of the Bible through distorting God's character and word, offering false but attractive promises if they would disobey God. Unlike Jesus, Adam and Eve gave in to this temptation and the results were devastating. For good reason Jesus describes Satan as "a murderer from the beginning ... a liar and the father of lies" (John 8 v 44).

Accusation: Satan, we are told in the Bible, is the "accuser of our brothers and sisters" (Revelation 12 v 10). The enemy employs a relentless whispering campaign, telling us we are unloved, unworthy and unforgivable. It is appropriate to feel guilt for sin. But unlike the conviction of the Holy Spirit, who brings us to faith in the cross, and restores our fellowship with God and gives us joy, Satan's desire is to lead us into despair, self-loathing and self-pity. And Satan wants us to be mini-accusers, too—he wants us to engage in accusation and gossip in order to tear apart the church from within.

Deception: Satan is called the deceiver and a liar. One of the ways in which he undermines the Christian's confidence in Christ and the gospel is through false teaching in the church, distorting the truth of the gospel. Paul calls teaching that happens in church but is not based on biblical truth "the trap of the devil" (2 Timothy 2 v 25-26).

Our defenses

The Bible is does not pull any punches: the Christian life is a spiritual battle, and the forces ranged against Christians are powerful. How should we respond?

Have confidence in the cross: It is vital to keep our confidence in what Jesus has done at the cross. Our victory has already been won for us when Jesus died for us. Jesus describes his crucifixion as the point at which "the prince of this world [was] driven out"—the place where the devil was defeated (John 12 v 31). In other words, through the cross, the enemy's hold over Christ's people comes to an end. Since we are forgiven people, there is now nothing the devil can rightly accuse us of. As Spirit-filled people, we are able to resist temptation. As Bible-believing people, we know and love what is true. Yes, we will continue to struggle with temptation and sin while we live on earth. But we now have a way out and the power to lives different lives through what God the Son accomplished on the cross and through the gift of God the Holy Spirit.

Put on spiritual armor: In Ephesians 6 v 10-18 Paul encourages believers to "put on the full armor of God" (v 11, 13). It's worth grabbing a Bible and reading about it. What we see is that the armour that protects us is the gospel itself; all we have received in Christ. Confessing our faith in what Christ has done, and reminding ourselves of this by reading the Scripture (the "sword of the Spirit," v 17) is the way to stand firm in this battle.

Develop counter strategies: What we must remember is that Satan knows our weaknesses and where we are vulnerable. Therefore we too must know our areas of weakness—and build counter strategies to keep us standing firm on the gospel.

When we are struggling with temptation, we need to develop a counter strategy of praising Jesus and singing a hymn. Why? Because the devil cannot bear hearing Jesus being praised! "Submit yourselves, then, to God. Resist the devil, and he will flee from you" (James 4 v 7).

When we are feeling oppressed and under spiritual attack—perhaps being tempted to believe the deceptive lies of the enemy that we are worthless, un-loved and alone—we need to stand on God's truth. Speak the Scriptures aloud and put your name in the verses! "But now, this is what the LORD says—he who created you, [your name!], he who formed you, [your name!]: 'Do not fear, for I have redeemed you; I have summoned you by name; you are mine ... When you pass through the rivers, they will not sweep over you. When you walk through the fire, you will not be burned ... Since you are precious and honored in my sight, and because I love you..." (Isaiah 43 v 1-2, 4).

Victory is won

We can do all this boldly and with courage because the cross is where sin—the flesh, the world and the devil—were ultimately defeated! But for now, the enemy still has limited freedom to tempt, deceive and accuse (which will only strength-en our faith when we respond in obedience). So we must stand our ground in the power of Jesus and all that he has accomplished. But on that final day when Jesus returns, the "great accuser" will be overthrown and evil will be removed finally and forever, "and so we will be with the Lord forever" (1 Thessalonians 4 v 17).

As I wrote in *Hope Has Its Reasons*: "Our lives can be lived well, with courage and with joy, because we live by the hope of the resurrection. So no matter what life drops in our laps, if we will only trust God and wait and never lose heart, the song we sing one day will be of victory. And then, with battles over, the time will come when faith becomes sight and hope fulfillment and our whole beings are united with the God we love. Joy of all joys, goal of our desire, all that we long for will be ours, for we will be his."

5. Talking About God Without Sounding Religious

John 4 v 5-30

Imagine how the disciples felt when they saw Jesus alive, raised from the dead. Luke tells us that they responded first in disbelief, then incredulity and finally overwhelming joy. *It was true! Jesus was who he said he was! He was alive!* (Luke 24 v 37-49).

What were they to do with this glorious message of good news? Jesus told them: "Repentance for the forgiveness of sins will be preached in [my] name to all nations, beginning at Jerusalem. You are witnesses of these things" (v 47-48).

Those men and women in Jerusalem faced a daunting responsibility. They had a job to do of utmost importance—and *so do we!* Perhaps that is why Jesus went on immediately to talk about the Holy Spirit: "I am going to send you what my Father has promised; but stay in the city until you have been clothed with power from on high" (v 49).

Jesus knew that to accomplish this task we need the power of the Spirit, who can take the message about Jesus and convert it into a glorious reality—both in our lives and the lives of others. What Jesus was saying in effect was this: *This is the message the world has been waiting for, and I am giving you the job of telling them! I am returning to heaven, from where I will equip and empower you. But my mission is now going to be accomplished through you!*

Yet in our politically correct age, is it possible to engage in the sensitive task of sharing the good news of Jesus without sounding preachy or "holier-than-thou"? Does it even work anymore?

We need to be encouraged and equipped for sharing the news about Jesus by seeing how Jesus himself did it when he was on earth. Let's look at how Jesus related with authenticity, compassion and truth to someone whose life was messy and whose beliefs were confused.

 Historical Context

Jesus was constantly criticized by the religious leaders for his association with "sinners." Religious people of Jesus' day thought it was fine to preach to unbelievers—but to befriend them, to eat meals together, to actually *enjoy* their company? That was unacceptable. In the passage we are about to read, Jesus reveals important principles about sharing our faith.

We will see Jesus do the inconceivable. In his culture it was considered the height of inappropriate behavior for a religious man to talk with a woman; but to speak to a woman of low moral standing was unthinkable.

Besides ignoring those social prejudices, Jesus also overlooked the deep racial and religious prejudice that Jews felt toward Samaritans. The orthodox Jews of Jesus' day looked on the Samaritans as a corrupt race because their Jewish ancestors had intermarried with another race. The Jews also despised the Samaritans for having a mixed religion, which accepted pagan idolatry with elements of Jewish faith. The feeling was mutual; the Samaritans often refused lodging to Jews passing through their territory. So Jews often traveled to the east side of the Jordan River to avoid Samaria. The bitterness between Jews and Samaritans was at its height in Jesus' day.

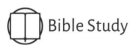 Bible Study

Read John 4 v 1-20

Jesus and his disciples have left the region of Judea and are passing through the Samaritan town of Sychar. It is midday and Jesus, being tired from the journey, rests at Jacob's well while the disciples go to get food.

In first-century middle-eastern culture, women would go to and from the well as a group. And because of the heat, they would go in the cool of the day, in the morning and evening.

1. This woman comes alone at midday to draw water. What does this suggest about her?

_____

_____

o Clearly something is very wrong, yet Jesus begins his conversation with her by sharing his personal need, rather than first addressing her problem. Why doesn't Jesus begin their conversation by first explaining who he is and why she needs his message, do you think (v 7)?

_____

_____

o What does this reveal about Jesus' understanding of human nature and of this woman in particular?

_____

_____

_____

2. Considering that he is tired, thirsty and hungry when she arrives at the well, how does Jesus' response reveal his compassion and what truly matters to him?

_____

_____

o Why is sharing our own need and being willing to receive from others one aspect of being an authentic witness for God?

_____

_____

_____

In verse 10, Jesus says: "If you knew the gift of God and who it is that asks you for a drink, you would have asked him and he would have given you living water." Samaritans would have understood "the gift of God" to be primarily the *Torah* of Moses (Samaritans accepted only the first five books of the Old Testament). But Jesus is saying something far more radical: that the supreme gift of God is found not in a book, but in a person—namely himself!

3. Describe the woman's reaction to Jesus' offer in verses 11-12. Do you think she understands what Jesus is offering?

_____

_____

_____

4. What does Jesus say about this "living water" that makes it so appealing to her (v 13-15)?

_____

_____

o Why is arousing curiosity an important skill in being a witness to Christ?

_____

_____

_____

Read John 4 v 16-30

5. This is a crucial point in the conversation. Just when the woman asks to receive this living water, Jesus suddenly delves into her personal life and asks her to go call her husband. Why do you think he brings up her list of past marriages and present problematic relationship (v 16-18)?

_____

_____

o What dangers are there when people respond to the Christian gospel without understanding what the Christian life entails?

_____

_____

_____

No doubt stunned by Jesus' prophetic knowledge of her personal life, she tries to change the topic to something "safer": the Jewish/Samaritan disagreement over where is the proper place to worship. Jesus not only treats her question seriously, but he reveals to her the most important teaching on worship in the entire New Testament.

6. What does Jesus teach about what constitutes true worship (v 22-24)?

_____

_____

_____

Most probably the woman responded with a sigh—hoping that one day the Messiah would come and bring clarity to all these questions (like the Jews, the Samaritans were also waiting for Messiah). Or perhaps she was beginning to wonder just who this stranger was! Then Jesus drops a bombshell: "I, the one speaking to you—I am he" (v 26).

7. Put yourself in her shoes now that she knows who Jesus is, and look back over their conversation. What difference would it make to realize that the one who has been speaking to her is actually the Messiah (v 26)?

_____

_____

_____

When the disciples returned with the food, they were stunned to find Jesus talking with a woman. In that day for Jesus to speak to a woman—even worse a Samaritan woman, and a woman of low moral standing—was not only shocking, it was unprecedented. Imagine how this woman felt, knowing that Jesus hadn't ignored her once the disciples arrived.

Read John 4 v 39-42

8. Describe the woman's message to the townspeople, and their response (v 28-30, 39-42).

_____

_____

Consider the impact that meeting Jesus had on her. No doubt she had come alone at midday to avoid the crowd of women pointing fingers and gossiping about her immoral life. But encountering Jesus, who knew all about her scandalous past, yet who treated her with respect and courtesy, freed her to race to the townspeople and acknowledge her greatest point of shame: "Come, see a man who told me everything I've ever done" (v 29).

9. The religious and respectable people of Jesus' day would have regarded this woman as a lost cause. Even his own disciples were shocked that Jesus was speaking to her. It is easy to look at people living immoral lives and assume they wouldn't be open to God.

What did Jesus see in her, and even in her moral history, that caused him to believe she would be open to God?

_____

_____

_____

 Live What You Learn

o _What can we learn from both Jesus and this woman about sharing our faith?_

o _This woman became the first evangelist in John's Gospel! How does it affect your attitude to others to know that Jesus considers no one a lost cause to God?_

o _What opportunities have you had to share your faith with someone who doesn't believe? How did it go?_

Following Jesus: Some Tips On Sharing Our Faith

- Remember that it's not about us; it's about God.

- Jesus makes us "fishers of men" as we follow him—he goes before us.

- Listen and ask good questions.

- The love of Christ, shown in his people, is what opens doors.

- You are one witness among many, and may be one link in a longer chain.

- We all have the same fears—be open and honest about them!

- Ask people to investigate Jesus by looking at the Bible.

- Share out of joy, not out of duty.

Life Stories

Praying Together

- Praise God for your salvation, and for how he sought you and never gave up! And for the friends who shared Christ with you!

- Ask for forgiveness for when you fear the opinion of others more than God's.

- Ask God to show you who he is seeking among your friends; to create in them a spiritual hunger, and for them to be willing to do a Seeker Bible study with you.

- Pray that you will be an effective witness to your friends; that they will see something in your life that makes them ask questions.

- Ask God to use you to lead one person to Christ this year.

You'll find some more books about the themes of this session on page 62.

↓ Going Deeper: Sharing Your Story

The good news of the gospel is how God sent his Son, Jesus, to reconcile the world to himself through his sacrifice on the cross. The gospel is specific truths about a specific person whom we proclaim. And God "has committed to us the message of reconciliation" (2 Corinthians 5 v 19). It's our God-given job, and responsibility, to tell the gospel story to everyone we can.

But we also have another story to tell—our story. For the Christian, the story of their life is the story of how the power of the gospel has worked in their life. To put it another way, our story is an illustration of the gospel's power—though it is not the gospel itself.

Our story is how God revealed Jesus to us; how he reached into our lives and began to change us. Because our story is about God's grace in our lives, it means every Christian's story is sacred. Furthermore, our story is uniquely ours; it cannot be duplicated or repeated. In one real sense, our story is unassailable—no one can deny or refute what God has done in our lives. Skeptics may argue with our arguments for God, but they cannot prove that our experience with God did not happen. Our story does not lose its power if we were raised in the church and have known Jesus since we were children, rather than if we were saved from a notorious life of sin. So there are times when explaining the gospel story by talking about our own story is more powerful and more helpful for someone than going straight to the gospel, or debating issues to do with its truth or content.

We must learn how to tell God's story. But we also need to learn how to tell our story. Many Christians don't know the precise date or time when God brought them into his kingdom. Conversion is a process that involves great mystery. Every story is different and displays God's immense creativity and grace in how he reaches each individual. But no matter how we finally crossed from death to life through faith in Jesus, all of our stories reveal a God who loves us, who reached in, who came through and who didn't abandon us. They show that only a power that is stronger than ourselves can help us to overcome ourselves.

In thinking about how to share your story with a person who doesn't yet know Christ, these prompts might be helpful. Consider writing down responses to the categories listed:

1. A little about my life before knowing Christ:

- o What was I like?

- o My most important value was...

- o My religious background and attitude toward Jesus was...

2. What God used to begin to open my eyes:

- o I was awakened to my need through... (people, books, circumstances, suffering, failure)

- o What I thought or noticed about myself at that point was...

3. How I came into my relationship with Christ:

- o Was it gradual or sudden, and what were the defining moments?

- o The aspects of the gospel that touched/persuaded me most were...

- o What were the reasons why the gospel had the ring of truth?

- o I saw my need was...

4. How Christ is affecting my life:

- o What changed was...

- o I'm still in process, but one way in which God is changing my life is...

Useful Resources

Session One: What Is God's Plan For My Life?

Romans 8 – 16 For You, chapters 1 – 3 (Tim Keller)

Calling (Os Guinness)

Children of the Living God (Sinclair Ferguson)

You Can Really Grow (John Hindley)

On the *Going Deeper* topic: *Loving The Way Jesus Loves* (Phil Ryken)

Session Two: Growing Together In Christ

True Worship (Vaughan Roberts)

Who on earth is the Holy Spirit? (Tim Chester)

Keep in Step With the Spirit (J.I. Packer)

Life Together in Christ (Ruth Haley Barton)

Session Three: Why Pray When We Can Worry Instead?

Too Busy Not to Pray (Bill Hybels)

Prayer: Experiencing Awe and Intimacy with God (Tim Keller)

Hearing God (Dallas Willard)

Listening Prayer (Leanne Payne)

A Praying Life (Paul Miller)

On the *Going Deeper* topic: *God's Big Picture* (Vaughan Roberts)

Session Four: Walking In Obedience

How People Change (Tim Lane & Paul Tripp)

A Long Obedience in the Same Direction (Eugene Peterson)

The Hole in our Holiness (Kevin DeYoung)

Respectable Sins (Jerry Bridges)

On the *Going Deeper* topic: *Did the Devil Make Me Do It?* (Mike McKinley)

Session Five: Talking About God Without Sounding Religious

Out of the Saltshaker (Becky Pippert)

Hope Has Its Reasons (Becky Pippert)

Honest Evangelism (Rico Tice)

Questioning Evangelism (Randy Newman)

LIVE | GROW | KNOW

Also available in the range:

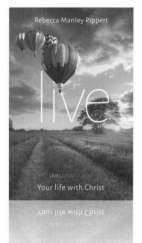

Live

In this first part of her series exploring the Christian life, Becky looks at what the gospel is and how we know it's true, what the Christian life is like, and how to start and keep going as a follower of Christ—how to really LIVE. Ideal for new Christians and not-yet-Christians as well as more longstanding believers. *With accompanying DVD and online downloads.*

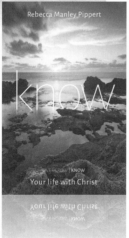

Know

What are the key beliefs of the Christian faith? How should we look at the world, and our own place in it? Over five sessions, Becky takes us through the core doctrines of Christianity, helping us KNOW what God wants us to know about ourselves, our world, and our future. *With accompanying DVD and online downloads.*

For more information, visit:
thegoodbook.com/livegrowknow
the goodbook.co.uk/livegrowknow

thegoodbook
COMPANY

Opening up the Bible

At The Good Book Company, we are dedicated to helping Christians and local churches grow. We believe that God's growth process always starts with hearing clearly what he has said to us through his timeless word—the Bible.

Ever since we opened our doors in 1991, we have been striving to produce resources that honor God in the way the Bible is used. We have grown to become an international provider of user-friendly resources to the Christian community, with believers of all backgrounds and denominations using our Bible studies, books, evangelistic resources, DVD-based courses and training events.

We want to equip ordinary Christians to live for Christ day by day, and churches to grow in their knowledge of God, their love for one another, and the effectiveness of their outreach.

Call us for a discussion of your needs or visit one of our local websites for more information on the resources and services we provide.

North America: www.thegoodbook.com
UK & Europe: www.thegoodbook.co.uk
Australia: www.thegoodbook.com.au
New Zealand: www.thegoodbook.co.nz

North America: 866 244 2165
UK & Europe: 0333 123 0880
Australia: (02) 6100 4211
New Zealand (+64) 3 343 1990